The Deep Woods' Business

uncollected translations from the Chinese

Arthur Cooper grew up in a small village near Oxford, studying Icelandic in his youth and turning to Far Eastern languages shortly before the War. He served in the Foreign Office from 1938 to 1968 and was involved in breaking Japanese codes for the Government Code and Cipher School. After his retirement he returned to a special interest in Chinese poetry and script. He published *Li Po and Tu Fu* (Penguin Classics) in 1973 and a monograph on *The Creation of the Chinese Script* (China Society) in 1978. Shortly before his death in 1988 he contributed to the *Oxford Companion to the Mind* and to the Penguin Classics volume *The Translator's Art*. What he completed of his work on *'Heart and Mind': Ancient Language-Making as Recorded in the Chinese Script* is presently being edited for publication.

When Arthur Cooper died on the 16th January 1988, the English language lost not its most prolific but, arguably, its finest translator from Chinese poetry since Arthur Waley.

Arthur Cooper

The Deep Woods' Business

uncollected
translations
from the Chinese
by
Arthur R V Cooper

wellsweep

ACKNOWLEDGEMENTS

Calligraphy on the title page and front cover, and accompanying ten of the poems, is by Joseph S P Lo.

The calligraphy accompanying two poems, 'Ode 11' and 'When I was Green' by Xin Qiji is in Arthur Cooper's own hand.

Cover design and original artwork is by Ivel Weihmüller.

Certain translations in this volume are reproduced with the kind permission of Penguin Books Ltd; *Renditions*, Hong Kong; and *Agenda*, London. Two poems were also reproduced in the *Elek Book of Oriental Verse*. Full details may be found in the notes.

This collection first published in 1990 by
Wellsweep Press
719 Fulham Road
London SW6 5UL

0 948454 09 1 trade edition (laminated cover)
0 948454 59 8 readers' edition (laid paper cover)

The publisher gratefully acknowledges the financial assistance of the Arts Council of Great Britain.

Designed and set by Wellsweep
Printed on recycled paper
by E & E Plumridge, Linton, Cambridge

dedicated by Diana Cooper
'to Arthur's friends'

Contents

Introduction

Arthur Cooper's *Li Po and Tu Fu*, translated for Penguin Classics, came as a revelation to both general readers of poetry and students of Chinese, and it delighted the small group of people who have brought these interests together. The combination of faithfulness to the poet's original sense with vital and *strict* poetic language in the translated version was all but unheard of. Since Arthur Waley, the translation of Chinese poetry had been relegated, on the one hand, to a few inspired but constrained academics, more or less unconcerned with the poetic vitality of their renditions, or, on the other, to poetic amateurs, visibly daunted by the immense demands of the Chinese language, forging ahead nonetheless in the footsteps of Ezra Pound. None of the latter have yet come near to the adaptions of that Modernist master—to his *Cathay* poems (and later, the less influential version of his *Book of Songs*) which, indisputably, changed the history and shape of English poetry. Cooper was, himself, sceptical of Pound's overall achievement, although he recognized the unique position of the *Cathay* poems. What is certain is that if Chinese verse is ever again to have a major influence on English poetry, some account will have to be taken of the small but disproportionately significant body of translations which Arthur Cooper left behind him.

While the same set of 'rules' could not be applied to Chinese originals written in irregular forms, Arthur Cooper's 'translation' of the syllabic and rhythmic form of five and seven syllable verse was particularly successful and is a good example of the benefits of such a procedure. Waley had allowed himself 'sprung rhythm' and tried to match the strong beats in his English lines with syllables in the Chinese. Cooper translated the Chinese syllabic metres into workable English equivalents while counting strictly and, most importantly, for the 'feel' of the original rhythm and its modulation of sense within the line. This permitted him to preserve an equivalent of the Chinese caesura which always comes three syllables before the line break. The five syllable line of two plus three becomes four plus five syllables in Cooper's English. The seven syllable line of four plus three, becomes six plus five. Cooper's lines—in this type of poem—are then split, with the short half indented and the second half without an initial capital, to further reveal the structure of the original. Finally he chose to end the first part of the line with a stressed syllable and the second with a stressed-unstressed pair. This approach was not, however, arbitrary. Cooper saw it as 'a good basic measure in English, able to suit a wide range of poems by taking colour from the syntax and from the content in meaning, as does the original ... Chinese metre that it represents.' (LPTF, p. 83) A great deal is still lost in such translation—rhyme, tonal patterning, the incredible concentration of meaning possible with literary Chinese (see the note for 'Ancient Air for the Lute' by Jiang Kui below), but it has the undoubted virtue of insisting on close, poetic attention to the language of the translated version.

If Arthur Cooper had done no more than fill out his well devised formal equivalents for Chinese metres, then the value of his work would still be in doubt. But Cooper was a poet and his translations achieve the status of poems in English, while fully acknowledging their origins.

It is said that Bai Juyi used to read what he had written to his maid and would cut out anything she couldn't understand on first hearing. Bai still, of course, wished to achieve a poetic density of meaning in the words he used as well as their opening out to an imaginative world beyond the words themselves, but he wanted to achieve this without sacrificing the everyday language of the people around him. Cooper had similar concerns and aspirations for his renditions, and he was largely successful.

Where the poem demanded it, Arthur Cooper was also inclined to explain any allusions or obscurities which the original contained. But somehow he managed to turn potentially daunting 'footnotes' into imaginative, short, essay-like explorations. The *Li Po and Tu Fu* volume is well served with such pieces and readers will find similar writing amongst the notes appended to the present book. *Li Po and Tu Fu* was also introduced by a long essay which will stand for some time as one of the best general introductions to Chinese poetry and one of the finest general treatments of its poetic in comparative technical terms.

Buried in this essay and in the notes accompanying the poems by Li and Du (Wade-Giles, Tu) were a number of versions by other poets. This is the source for some of the poems in this book—now extracted from this subordinate context and given the prominence they deserve. Other translations are reproduced from their publication in magazines which are now quite difficult to obtain. A few of the translations here are published for the first time. The aim is to bring together all of Cooper's verse translation, other than the Li and Du poems forming the backbone of the Penguin Classics volume.

On retirement and after returning to his study of Chinese, Arthur Cooper became fascinated by the problems of the unique characteristics and early development of the Chinese script. His work on this subject was unfinished at the time of his death, but had already attracted some attention and is presently being edited for publication. Some of us have regretted the fact that this later concentration prevented Cooper from translating more poetry and, in particular, it is sad that he never produced a new version of the *Shi Jing* or *Book of Odes* (see his essay on the difficulties of achieving this in *The Translator's Art*). He saw his work on the script as an essential prerequisite—and so it may prove to be—but the lack of more versions from this Chinese 'classic of poetry' by a poet and scholar eminently qualified to render it into English is a great loss.

Two quotations will conclude these brief introductory remarks—some words singled out by Arthur Cooper on the particular qualities of Chinese poetry, and a few further words of his own treating the same subject. He was especially fond of this quotation from the French sinologist and translator, Paul Demiéville,

> 'A poem of twenty syllables could hardly be a great poem? But wait! Each of these syllables is a little world in itself, a linguistic cell irradiated with meanings like a faceted jewel. It throws out powerful resonances to both ear and eye, for it is written by means of a 'calligram', which is itself a work of art, and its pronunciation has subtle modulations that play their part in the prosody. Thus it can touch aesthetic sensibilities in centres of the mind hereditarily given such exercise, for which our psychology and our physiology seem scarcely to have an equivalent ... Everywhere, beneath the ever concrete words themselves you will perceive the immensity of the Chinese heaven and earth—a universe responsive to Man—and also the silent resonance of profundities which slip the net of language. Little by little you will rediscover yourself in a world of enchantment, where all is tranquillity, simplicity, ease; and besides which all other poetry will seem verbose.'

> 'That my translation falls short of the originals is inevitable, but I believe that Chinese poetry, even in translation, can retain something of its original great quality ... of appeal to the mental eye. There's much akin to Chinese painting in the way this is achieved, by great

economy and the leaving of space. In some ways a poem is a vessel—for the reception of the imagination, rather than for its instruction.'

John Cayley
September 1990

Note on the Texts

The texts of translations published here follow the most recently published versions where these are available. For certain poems, significant variations are recorded, and selected examples are quoted in full in the notes, giving the reader a glimpse of the translation process, before the finished version—never final or entirely satisfactory—is arrived at.

Where a particular translation or note has been previously published, the original system of romanisation—normally Wade-Giles—has been retained in the text. However, in the editor's notes, headings, table of contents, authors' names, titles re-translated for this collection, etc., the Pinyin system has been adopted, and in quoted notes the Pinyin is also given in square brackets.

The Deep Woods' Business

關、雎鳩在之河洲窈窕淑女君子好
逑　參差荇菜左右流之窈窕
淑女寤寐求之求之不得寤寐思服
悠哉〻〻輾轉反側參差荇菜左右采之
窈窕淑女琴瑟友之參差荇菜左右
芼之窈窕淑女鐘鼓樂之

Ode 1: Kuan Ch'ü

Waterbirds on
River islands:
Shy the Nymph our
Shepherd's chosen!

Waterlilies
Wreathe around her:
Shy the Nymph he
Waking, sleeping
Never reaches;
Waking, sleeping,
Longing, longing,
Turning, tossing!

Water lilies
To adorn her:
Shy the Nymph we
Greet with zither,

Water lilies
To array her:
To the shy Nymph
Bell, drum bring glee!

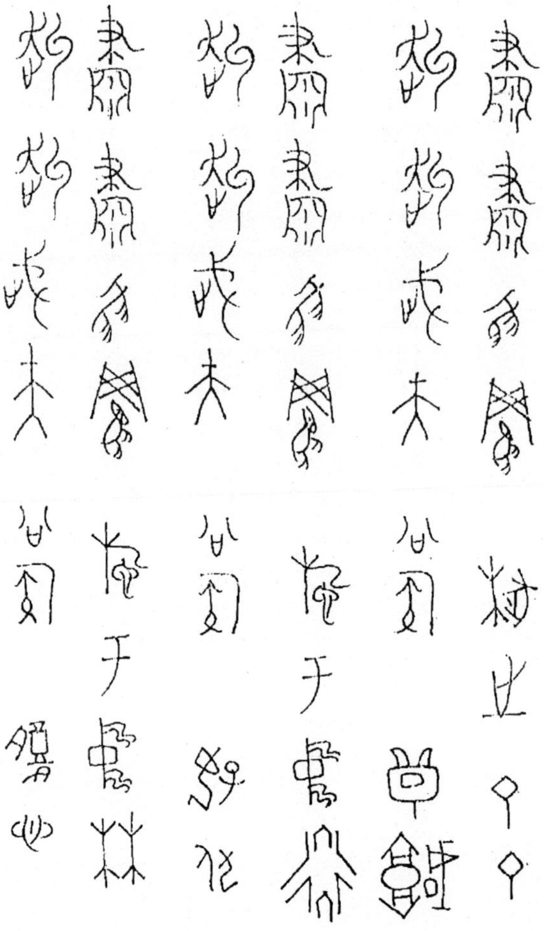

Ode 11

Ware, ware, snares for hares,
   Peg 'em down, ding, ding:

   Fair, fair, the Warriors,
      My Lord's
   Bucklers and Bastions!

Ware, ware, snares for hares,
   Spread 'em in the tracks:

   Fair, fair, the Warriors,
      My Lord's
   Dearest companions!

Ware, ware, snares for hares,
   Spread 'em in the woods:

   Fair, fair, the Warriors,
      My Lord's
   Soul and opinions!

匏有苦葉
濟有深涉

深則厲
淺則揭

有瀰濟盈
有鷕雉鳴

濟盈不濡軌
雉鳴求其牡

雝雝鳴鴈
旭日始旦

士如歸妻
迨冰未泮

招招舟子
人涉卬否
人涉卬否
卬須我友

Ode 34

He: 'The Gourd now sprouts its bitter blade:
The ford is now too deep to wade!'

She: 'Where it is deep there are stepping stones,
Where it is shallow just raise your clothes!'

He: 'But see how the raging waters fall,
And hark to the pheasant's grating call!'

She: 'You could still cross with your axle dry!
That was the pheasant's mating cry.

Riverbirds mingle their voices now
As a new sun rises over the brow,

But he who would bring a bride to his bed
Should never wait till the frosts have fled!

Beckons and beckons the boatman aboard:
Let others cross but no, not I,
Let others cross but no, not I,
I shall await my love and lord!'

有狐綏、在彼淇梁心之
憂矣之子無裳　有狐
綏、在彼淇厲心之憂矣
之子無帶　有狐綏、
在彼淇側心之憂矣之子
無服

Ode 63

That fox creeps creeps
Along the bank ...
Oh, my heart's grief!
This lordling has
No robes of rank.

That fox creeps creeps
Across the ford ...
Oh, my heart's grief!
No girdle has
this youthful lord.

That fox creeps creeps
Now over there ...
Oh, my heart's grief!
This youth has nothing
Fit to wear.

彼采葛兮
一日不見
如三月兮

彼采蕭兮
一日不見
如三秋兮

彼采艾兮
一日不見
如三歲兮

Ode 72

There, gathering a kind of artemisia, oh!
One day not see
Like three months, oh!

There gathering another kind of artemisia, oh!
One day not see
Like three autumns, oh!

There gathering yet another kind of artemisia, oh!
One day not see
Like three years, oh!

客從遠方來遺我一端
綺相去萬餘里故人
心尚爾文彩雙鴛鴦裁
為合歡被著以長相思
緣以結不解以膠投漆
中誰能別離此

From the *Nineteen Old Poems*

From far away
did a Guest appear
And give to me
a bolt of silk.

So though he's gone
a thousand miles,
I know my Love's
heart is still near!

I'll broider it
with a brace of ducks ...

河中之水歌　　梁武帝

河中之水向東流
洛陽女兒名莫愁
莫愁十三能織綺
十四采桑南陌頭
十五嫁爲盧家婦
十六生兒字阿侯
盧家蘭室桂爲梁
中有鬱金蘇和香
頭上金釵十二行
足下絲履五文章

Liang Wudi (464–549)

The Waters in the Rivers

The waters in the rivers
  all Eastward flow,
At Loyang was a maiden
  by name Mo-ch'ou:

Mo-ch'ou when she was thirteen,
  could weave and sew
At fourteen pick mulberry leaves
  South on the row,

So at fifteen was wedded
  to Mr Lou,
At sixteen was child-bedded,
  a boy, Ah Hou ...

The Lous have pavilions
  with roofs so fair,
Saffron and liquidambar
  perfume the air,

And she has twelve gold hairpins
  put in her hair,
For her feet brocade slippers
  are hers to wear:

珊瑚挂鏡爛生光
平頭奴子擎履箱
人生富貴何所望
恨不早嫁東家王

In coral hangs her mirror
    all gleaming, where
The caskets with these slippers
    neat handmaids bear ...

In a life of such splendour
    what could be wrong?
She still would she'd been wed to
    East neighbour Wang!

醉中作　　張説

醉後無窮樂
彌勝未醉時
動容皆是舞
出語總成詩

Zhang Yue (667–730)

Written While Drunk

  Once drunk I make
Music unending
  (Even better
Than when I'm sober);

  All my movements
Are simply Ballet,
  Can't even Speak
But it's a poem!

春眠不觉晓处
处闻啼鸟夜来
风雨声花落
知多少

孟浩然

春晓

Meng Haoran (689–740)

Spring Awakening

In Spring one sleeps
absent to morning
Then everywhere
hears the birds singing:

After all night
the voice of the storm
And petals fell—
who knows how many?

過香積寺　　王維

不知香積寺
數里入雲峰
古木無人逕
深山何處鐘
泉聲咽危石
日色冷青松
薄暮空潭曲
安禪制毒龍

On Going by the Shrine of Stored Incense

Where does it lie,
Shrine of Stored Incense,
How many miles
into cloudy peaks?

Where ancient woods
have no tracks of men
Deep in the mountains
sounds somewhere a bell;

Waterfall's voice
coming from steep crags
And sun's colour
cold on the larches,

A pale stillness
erasing lake's rim,
Meditation
tames Deadly Dragon!

君自故鄉來
應知故鄉事
來日綺窗前
寒梅著花未

王維詩

Lines

You that have come
from my old village,
You ought to know
all the village news:

The early plum
before my window,
Was it in bloom
by the day you left?

送別　　王維

山中相送罷
日暮掩柴扉
春草明年綠
王孫歸不歸

On My Mountain

On my mountain
I have said good-bye,
As the sun set
closed my wattle gate:

But the Spring grass
will be green next year,
Won't Your Honour
visit me again?

空山不见人但
闻人语响返景
入深林复照青
苔上

王维 鹿柴

On Empty Slopes

On empty slopes
we see nobody,
Yet we can hear
men's echoed phrases:

Retreating light
enters the deep woods
And shines again
on the green mosses.

日夕見寒山便
爲獨往客不知
深林事但有麏
麚跡

裴迪
鹿柴

Pei Di (8th century)

As the Day Fades

As the day fades
see the cold mountain,
Suppose us those
travellers alone:

We'd never know
the deep woods' business,
Only traces
of a stag or doe.

放魚　　白居易

曉日提竹籃　家童買春蔬
青青芹蕨下　疊臥雙白魚
無聲但呀呀　以氣相照濡
傾籃寫地上　撥剌長尺餘
豈惟刀機憂　坐見螻蟻圖
脱泉雖已久　得水猶可蘇
放之小池中　且用救乾枯
水小池窄狹　動尾觸四隅
一時幸苟活　久遠將何如
憐其不得所　移放於南湖
南湖連西江　好去勿踟躕
施思即望報　吾非斯人徒
不須泥沙底　辛苦覓明珠

Bai Juyi (772–846)

On Releasing Fish

When one morning, armed with a basket
I'd sent my boy to buy me spring greens,
Beneath the green green of the parsley
Were tucked away a pair of white fish:
They had no voice, yet with their 'O! O!'
They made their breath mutual moistening;
And when the load was tipped on the ground,
Smacked and slapped out (to more than a foot!)—
Now for far worse than the board and knife,
Helpless they saw the schemes of some ants!

Though long parted from their running brooks,
Given water they could still be fresh:
I let them loose in a little pond
I thought it might serve to salve their dryness;
Little water, and the pond confined,
They waved their tails and met its corners—
For one moment had a taste of life,
Longer, further, how could they manage?

I felt pity for their frustration,
Took them instead to the Southern Lake:
'The Southern Lake joins the West River,
So fare you well, please don't hesitate:
Doing good turns for sake of reward?
Of course I'm not that sort of fellow—
You mustn't, down in the mud and sand,
Trouble yourselves by searching for pearls!'

放旅雁　　白居易

九江十年冬大雪
江水生冰樹枝折
百鳥無食東西飛
中有旅雁聲最飢
雪中啄草冰上宿
翅冷騰空飛動遲
江童持網捕將去
手攜入市生賣之
我本北人今譴謫
人鳥雖殊同是客

On Releasing a Migrant Goose

At Kiukiang, the year Ten,
  that winter's blizzard,
The Yangtse waters froze
  and branches splintered:

Birds without food had flown
  Eastward and Westward,
But one, a migrant goose,
  cried the hungriest ...

In snow it pecked for grass,
  on ice it rested,
With frozen wings aspired,
  then rose too slowly:

A river boy with net
  caught it and took it,
Clutching it in his arms,
  alive to market ...

I was a Northern man,
  now I am banished,
Though bird and man unlike,
  alike we're strangers;

見此客鳥傷客人
贖汝放汝飛入雲
雁雁汝飛向何處
第一莫飛西北去
淮西有賊討未平
百萬甲兵久屯聚
官軍賊軍相守老
食盡兵窮將及汝
健兒飢餓射汝喫
拔汝翅翎爲箭羽

Seeing this stranger bird
   wounds a man stranger—
I'll ransom, set you free,
   fly to the clouds, bird!

Wild goose, wild goose, you fly
   in what direction?
Now, above all, don't fly
   Westward and Northward!

The Rebels West of Huai
   are not subdued yet,
A million armoured men
   long concentrated,

Both Crown and Rebel troops,
   grow old in stalemate;
Food gone, the wretched men
   are sure to get you:

Those 'sturdy lads', who starve,
   will shoot to eat you,
Pluck feathers from your wings
   and fletch their arrows!

夜雪　　白居易

已訝衾枕冷
復見窗戶明
夜深知雪重
時聞折竹聲

You've Just Said O

You've just said O!
at your cold pillow
When you notice
light on the window:

So deep the night,
snow must be lying;
Hark and again
at bamboos breaking!

花非花　　白居易

花非花霧非霧
夜半來天明去
來如春夢不多時
去似朝雲無覓處

Flower or Not Flower?

Flower or not flower; mist or not mist was here—
At midnight, came—with day, no longer there!
Came, as a dream of spring, a time;
Went, like a cloud at dawn, no where.

千山鸟飞绝
万径人踪灭孤
舟蓑笠翁独钓
寒江雪

柳宗元 江雪

Liu Zongyuan (773–819)

River Snow

Among mountains
where birds fly no more
Nor have the paths
any men's tracks now,

There's orphan boat
and old straw-hat man
Alone fishing
the cold river snow.

松下問童子言師
採藥去只在此山中
雲深不知處

賈島　尋隱者不遇

Jia Dao (777–841)

On Visiting a Hermit and Not Finding Him

Under a pine
I asked his pupil
Who said: 'Master's
gone gathering balm

Only somewhere
about the mountain:
The cloud's so thick
that I don't know where.'

聞樂天授江州司馬　　元稹

殘燈無焰影幢幢
此夕聞君謫九江
垂死病中驚坐起
暗風吹雨入寒窗

Yuan Zhen (779–831)

On Hearing of Bai Juyi's Exile and Relegation to the Post of District Officer at Jiujiang

A low lamp showed no flame
  but looming shadow,
Tonight came news of you
  at Kiukiang, banished;

Though ill and near to death
  I sat up startled:
A dark wind blew in rain
  through the cold window.

清明　　杜牧

清明時節雨紛紛
路上行人欲斷魂
借問酒家何處有
牧童遙指杏花村

Du Mu (803–852)

Ch'ing Ming

In Easter's cleansing rain,
    blown confusedly,
Traveller on the road
    (getting desparate)

Enquires if there's an inn
    in the neighbourhood?
Shepherd boy points to far
    Apricot Village.

君问归期未有期巴
山夜雨涨秋池何
当共剪西窗烛却
话巴山夜雨时

李商隐 夜雨寄北

Li Shangyin (813–858)

Letter North to His Wife

You ask when I return?
I have no date yet
(On Pa Mountains night rain
spreads pools of Autumn)

When we can snuff the light
in our west window
And talk of the night rains
on the Pa Mountains.

題僧壁　　李商隱

捨身求道有前蹤
乞腦剜身結願重
大去便應欺粟顆
小來兼可隱針鋒
蚌胎未滿思新桂
琥珀初成憶舊松
若信貝多真事語
三生同聽一樓鐘

Written on a Monastery Wall

To leave life, seek the Way,
  follow the others,
Which asks much, begs the brain,
  hollows the body;

Great gone, to see the World
  a grain of millet,
Small comes, to make it fit
  the Mystic Pinpoint:

Oysters, their wombs unfilled,
  long for the full moon,
And amber until made
  sighs for its past pine;

But faith in Holy Writ
  for the true message
Hears Present, Future, Past
  all in one gongstroke!

漁夫　二首　　李煜

浪花有意千重雪
桃李無言一隊春
一壺酒
一竿身
世上如儂有幾人

一櫂春風一葉舟
一綸繭縷一輕鉤
花滿渚
酒滿甌
萬頃波中得自由

Li Yu (937–978)

The Old Fisherman
Two Verses

If the wave-crests had their will,
How deep would be their snow
Here where the peach and plum
Are Spring's mute bodyguard:
        One pot of wine,
        One rod and line,
How many in the world
Are rich as countryfolk?

One pole in a Spring wind,
One leaf of a boat,
And one weightless hook:
        Flowers fill the isles,
        Wine fills his bowl,
Here among the tumbling waves
Freedom can be found!

黃梅時節　　司馬光

黃梅時節家家雨
青草池塘處處蛙
有約不來過夜半
閒敲棋子落燈花

Sima Guang (1019–1086)

He Said

Season of yellow plum
    and rain in gardens,
From green grass, ditch and dam
    frogs begin croaking:

He said ... but hasn't come
    and it's past midnight;
Chessmen I idly drum,
    the candle fading ...

元日　　王安石

爆竹聲中一歲除
春風送暖入屠蘇
千門萬戶曈曈日
總把新桃換舊符

Wang Anshi (1021–1086)

New Year's Day

In the firecrackers' din
    a year's extinguished:
Spring breezes will bring warmth
    to New Year wassail,

On shutters and on doors
    the sun shines brightly,
New mottoes on them all
    in place of old ones.

出郊　王安石

川原一片綠交加
深樹冥冥不見花
風日有情無處著
初回光景到桑麻

THE RIVER PLAINS ARE GREEN

The river plains are green
crossing and added,
Too dense and deep the trees
to see the flowers:

For their love sun nor breeze
find a fit object
Until the change of scene
to hemp and mulberry!

少年 其二

少年聽雨歌樓上紅燭昏羅帳
壯年聽雨客舟中江闊雲低
斷雁叫西風
而今聽雨僧廬下鬢已星星也
悲歡離合總無情一任階前
點滴到天明

When I Was Green

To the tune: *Chounu'er*

When I was green and hadn't seen
The bitterness of sorrows,
And upper floors
I loved to gain:
And upper floors
I loved to gain,
To put in odes, *très à la mode,*
My sorrows, I sought 'em.

Now all there's been, so that I've seen
The bitterness of sorrows,
I long to tell,
But I refrain:
I long to tell,
But I refrain,
And only say: 'Cooler today,
Quite a nip of Autumn!'

聽雨　　虞美人　　蔣捷

少年聽雨歌樓上
紅燭昏羅帳
壯年聽雨客舟中
江闊雲低
斷雁叫西風
而今聽雨僧廬下
鬢已星星也
悲歡離合總無情
一任階前
點滴到天明

Zhang Jie (1245–1310)

When I Was Green
To the tune: *Yu Meiren*

When I was green I'd hear the rain
On high in pleasure palaces,
Red candleglow on silk curtains;
Then in my prime I'd hear the rain
In ships with other passengers:
Thronged riverflow and clouds hanging,
Broken cries of wild geese in the Westerlies!

Now that once more, I hear the rain,
It's down in leaky monasteries;
Scattered stars show in my temples,
Meeting and parting, joy and pain
Have alike become meaningless:
Let it drip so without ceasing,
Patter on the steps outside until daybreak!

醉吟商小品　　姜夔

又正是春歸
細柳暗黃千縷
暮鴉啼處
夢逐金鞍去
一點芳心休訴
琵琶解語

Jiang Kui (1155?–1221?)

Air for the Lute

And so now Spring ends:
Willows weave yellow strands,
Cry evening crows.

Your gold saddlebow
Dreams, not words, follow now:
Those my lute knows!

雪梅

雪梅爭春未肯降
騷人閣筆費評章
梅須遜雪三分白
雪卻輸梅一段香
有梅無雪不精神
有雪無詩俗了人
日暮成詩天大雪
與梅並作十分春

Anonymous (13th century)

Snow and Plum

When Snow and Plum at Spring
contend for favour,
A poet shelves his brush
or wastes his paper!

For whiteness Snow beats Plum
and leads by Thirty;
Then Plum, for Scent, makes Snow
concede the Tourney:

But as Plum without Snow
lacks half the wonder
And Snow without a song
makes men look vulgar,

By Sunset I'd made this
(the snow still tumbled)
To show, with Plum, the Spring
has made a Hundred!

七律二首　其二

毛澤東

春風楊柳萬千條
六億神州盡舜堯
紅雨隨心翻作浪
青山著意化爲橋
天連五嶺銀鋤落
地動三河鐵臂搖
借問瘟君欲何往
紙船明燭照天燒

Mao Zedong (1893–1976)

FAREWELL TO THE GOD OF PLAGUES

1st July 1958

I had read in the issue of 30th June of The People's Daily News *that in Yüchiang District they had exterminated the blood-sucking parasite. One after another, floating thoughts were wafted through my mind, so that when night came I was unable to sleep. But when a light breeze, sweeping in warmth, and the rising sun approached my window, out into the distance I gazed at the southern skies; and, joyously, I took command of my brush!*

Spring winds move willow wands
   in tens of millions:
Six hundred million we
   shall all be Sage-Kings!

Our red rain to the mind
   translates as torrents,
Green hilltops are at will
   turned into bridges:

So, silver spades, sink sky-
   scraping Five Ranges,
And, iron arms, sway earth-
   quaking Three Rivers:

Tell us please, Prince of Plagues,
   Your choice of Journey?
Candles and paper boats
   blaze the skies for you!

十六字令三首　其一

毛澤東

山

快馬加鞭未下鞍

驚回首

離天三尺三

Mao Zedong (1893–1976)

Over Fells So High

Over fells so high
On a spirited horse, don't dismount,
Let the whip fly!
Then look back alarmed:
By three foot three you missed the sky!

Bibliography and Notes

Poems contained in this collection have appeared in the following publications:

'Seven poems translated from the Chinese', *Agenda*, Vol. 12, No. 2 (Summer 1974) pp. 53-67 (A74)
'From the Shi King', *Agenda*, Vol. 12, No. 4—Vol. 13, No. 1 (Winter-Spring 1975) pp. 66-67 (A75)
'Six Chinese Poems', *Agenda*, Vol. 16, No. 2 (Summer 1978) pp. 14-25 (A78)
'Ode 63', *Agenda*, Vol. 20, No. 3-4 (Autumn-Winter 1982-83) p. 60 (A82/1)
'Englishing the earliest Chinese poems', ibid., pp. 54-59 (A82/2)
Keith Bosley ed., *The Elek Book of Oriental Verse*, London: Paul Elek, 1979 (EBOV)
Arthur Cooper, *The Creation of the Chinese Script*, China Society Occasional Papers, No. 20. London: China Society, 1978 (CCS)
Li Po and Tu Fu: poems selected and translated with an introduction and notes by Arthur Cooper, Harmondsworth: Penguin, 1973. Some revisions were incorporated in reprintings from 1981. (LPTF)
'Six Poems', *Renditions: A Chinese-English translation magazine*, Nos. 21 & 22 (Spring & Autumn 1984), Special Issue: Poetry and Poetics, pp. 179-186 (Nb: This issue of *Renditions* was also published in book form under the title, *A Brotherhood in Song: Chinese poetry and poetics*, edited by Stephen C Soong, Hong Kong: Renditions, 1985.) (R84)
'The Oldest Chinese Poetry', in William Radice and Barbara Reynolds ed., *The Translator's Art: Essays in honour of Betty Radice*, Harmondsworth: Penguin, 1987 (TA)

The abbreviations in parentheses above are used in the following notes to indicate the sources of texts and also of variants where appropriate and necessary.

Introduction: The first part of the quotation from Demiéville—from the introduction to his *Anthologie de la poésie chinoise classique* (Éditions Gallimard, 1962)—is quoted and translated by Cooper in LPTF, p. 84. The second part is translated here by the editor from its quotation in an unpublished prose work amongst Cooper's papers. To the quotation in LPTF, the following note is appended, 'I am sure that Professor Demiéville is right in stressing this ['calligram' itself a work of art] as an integral part of a Chinese poem in the original; though many scholars and critics have reacted against what they have felt to be the excessive attention, also rather wrongly based, it has been given by some.'

The quotation from Cooper himself is transcribed from the recording of a broadcast he made for the BBC Third Programme, 'A Chinese Window on the Seasons'.

Ode 1: LPTF p. 49. In the first printings of the Penguin book, an earlier version of the translation is printed, which is given in its entirety here:

'Kuan-kuan!' birds on
River islands!
Shy the Nymph our
Shepherd's chosen.

Water lilies
Wreathe around her:
Shy the Nymph he
Waking, sleeping
Never reaches;
Waking, sleeping,
Longing, longing,
Turning, tossing.

Water lilies
To adorn her:
Shy the Nymph we
Greet with zither,

Water lilies
To array her:
To the shy Nymph
Bell, drum bring glee!

There is also a 'somewhat closer translation' in TA, p. 60-61:

'Guan, guan!' Ospreys
On the island,
Shy the Nymph our
Shepherd's chosen!

Water Gentians
Strew around her,
Shy the Nymph he
Waking, sleeping,
Never reaches,
Waking, sleeping,
Longing, longing,
Turning, tossing!

Water Gentians
Harvest for her,
Shy the Nymph we
Greet with zither,
Water Gentians
To array her,
For the shy Nymph
Bell, drum make glee!

Other variants exist in a version entitled 'Epithalamium' and prepared with Laurence Picken for a programme of 'Two ancient Chinese airs for the lute', but these are of less significance without the context of Picken and Cooper's accompanying correspondence.

Ode 11: A75; EBOV, p. 28. The text opposite the translation is in Arthur Cooper's own calligraphy and was published with the translation along with this note: 'The ancient script opposite is largely in the Oracle Bone style from 15th to 11th century BC (but some characters are from bronzes rather later). To follow the poem in the original read down the columns starting from the right: 4th character is "snare" (a net with a hare in it).'

Ode 34: A82/2, pp. 57-58.

Ode 63: A82/1. Cooper produced another version, published in TA, p. 51, '... the nearest I can as a word-for-word translation in English monosyllables ...':

There's fox creeps creeps
on yon Qi dam:
heart the grief oh!
The childe lacks robe.

There's fox creeps creeps
on yon Qi ford:
heart the grief oh!
The childe lacks belt.

There's fox creeps creeps
on yon Qi side:
heart the grief oh!
The childe lacks costume.

Ode 72: Previously unpublished and perhaps translated somewhat 'tongue in cheek', though clearly demonstrating the extreme simplicity of many of the Odes.

From the Nineteen Old Poems: LPTF, p. 242. The translation is of only the first part of the poem. The entire poem is, however, given in the accompanying calligraphy.

The Waters in the Rivers: LPTF, pp. 65-66. An earlier version, amongst Cooper's papers, translates the name of the poem's protagonist as 'Don't-cry-so'.

Written While Drunk: Previously unpublished.

Spring Awakening: LPTF, p. 111.

On Going by the Shrine of Stored Incense: LPTF, p. 94.

Lines: A78, p. 14.

On My Mountain: Previously unpublished.

On Empty Slopes & As the Day Fades: A74, p. 53, CCS, p. 40. The first of these two poems is a famous quatrain from an almost equally famous set of twenty such poems, the 'Wang River Sequence' *(Wangchuan ji)*, which Wang Wei wrote for specific sites on his estate. Chinese poets often wrote 'replies' to their fellows' works, and Wang Wei's friend, Pei Di wrote matching poems for each of those in Wang's sequence. These two poems form one pair from the set, which Arthur Cooper seems to have used as an image for his later work on the early Chinese script. Publication in A74 was accompanied by the following note; 'In P'ei Ti's [Pei Di] poem "travellers alone" is a Buddhist phrase for what we all are. "Stag and doe" in the original is two species of deer, but serving as a reminder of the lines in a poem of the 2nd century BC:

> White deer, roebuck and horned deer
> Now leap and now stand poised.
>
> (*Ch'u Tz'u, The Songs of the South,*
> David Hawkes, Oxford, 1959)'

On Releasing Fish & On Releasing a Migrant Goose: A74, pp. 55-59; R84, pp. 180-183. The following 'translator's note' accompanied these two poems in the *Renditions* issue:

'On Releasing Fish' and 'On Releasing a Migrant Goose': to release captive creatures was an act of piety, but both these poems are also political satires, written by Po Chü-i [Bai Juyi] in AD 815 on arrival at Kiukiang [Jiujiang], his place of banishment after being a close adviser to the Emperor (for whose ears they were clearly intended). In their hidden meaning, the two fish were himself and his great friend and fellow poet, Yuan Chen [Zhen], who had been similarly banished elsewhere; the 'mutual moistening', the sad poems on the plight they privately exchanged; and the ants, of course, those responsible for their banishment—than which death by the executioner's sword, but at the Emperor's command, would have been better, according to the poet (who had, in truth, been given light duties, without loss of pay, but far from the capital; and he was able to write much poetry). His contempt for his accusers was, however, justified: not daring to charge him with the advice, against their interests, he had given the Emperor, a duty in which he was protected, they had charged him with moral unsuitability for the court; on the grounds that after his mother had fallen into a well when picking flowers, he had praised both flowers and wells in his poems! Without direct allusion to it, the poet treats this trumped-up charge as it deserves: it happens that the Confucian Patron Saint of Filial Piety one day rescued two cranes wounded by hunters, healed them and released them; whereupon they flew back to him, each bearing a valuable pearl in its beak. In 'On Releasing a Migrant Goose', the poet is more serious and touches on one of the real reasons for his banishment: his opposition to a war against the 'rebels West of Huai', which had dragged on (to the profit, he claimed, only of the generals who were for-ever promising victory) but which he did not believe that the Imperial forces could win.

An earlier version of 'On Releasing Fish' shows the extensive revision to which Arthur Cooper subjected his versions. This was amongst his 'poetry course papers':

When one morning taking a basket
My household boy had gone for spring greens,
Beneath the green green of the parsley
Lay embracing a pair of white fish
That had no voice, a silent O! O!
Making their breath mutual moistening;
But basket load then tipped on the ground,
Smacked and slapped out, each more than a foot:

Isn't it worse than the kitchen knife
In vain to see the scheming of ants?

Though missing streams already too long,
Given water they might be revived
So I loosed them in a little pond
Serving at least to ease their dryness;
Water little and the pond confined,
A flick of tails brushed the four corners:

A moment's joy of the taste of life!
Longer, further, how to be managed?

I pitied them for this frustration,
Loosed them instead in the Southern Lake:
'The Southern Lake joins the West River,
So fare you well, don't stop politely;
Doing good turns for sake of reward,
It's not that I'm THAT sort of fellow:

You mustn't, down in the mud and sand,
Put yourself out with searching for PEARLS!'

You've Just Said O: LPTF, p. 83.

Flower or Not Flower?: A78, p. 22.

River Snow: LPTF, p. 140.

On Visiting a Hermit and Not Finding Him: LPTF, p. 106.

On Hearing of Bai Juyi's Exile and Relegation to the Post of District Officer at Jiujiang: LPTF, p. 82.

Ch'ing Ming: A78, p. 16, which has this note: 'Ch'ing Ming [Qingming] is the Chinese Easter, Spring Festival at about the same time, when people journey to visit family graves.'

Letter North to His Wife: A78, p. 20.

Written on a Monastery Wall: LPTF, p. 95-96.

The Old Fisherman: A74, p. 61. Written about 974. A74 includes the following note: '... Li Hou-chu [Houzhu], "Li the Last" ruler of the blood of the T'ang [Tang] emperors, though only of a tiny "empire" until he was deposed by the Sung [Song]: a helpless creature politically, but quite otherwise as a poet.'

He Said: A78, p. 18. Cooper's 'poetry course papers' have the following note relating to this poem: 'Another visual pun, in 'chessmen I idly drum': *xian qiao qi zi*. The last poem on this page, 'On visiting a Hermit ...' [see above] is one of the most famous in the language and by a poet who worked so hard at his poems that each New Year he sacrificed to them and asked them to restore the energy they had taken. Once, riding a donkey, he was composing and trying to decide between 'knock on a moonlit door' and 'push on a moonlit door', gesticulating the two when he knocked over a high official. 'Knock/push' is now a term for working at a poem, but men the door and yue, the moon, form xian the word by chance or 'idly' in Sima Guang's poem, where 'drum' is 'knock', but also, since this poem, 'to try' (at chess).'

New Year's Day: Previously unpublished. From a Christmas/New Year's card.

The River Plains Are Green: Previously unpublished.

When I Was Green: A74, p. 63; EBOV, p. 46; R84, p. 185.

When I Was Green: A74, p. 65; R84, p. 184. a74 has the following note relating to this and the previous poem: 'Hsin Ch'i-chi [Xin Qiji] in the 12th century ... was a great political leader and resistance hero against the Tartars, as well as one of the greatest of all the *tz'u* [*ci*] poets. In his poem "upper floors" means fashionable places (which were always upstairs) with wine, food, music, poetry and girls: the "pleasure palaces" of the next poem, which was written in homage to his in the next century; after the night of the Mongol conquest had fallen. Now Buddhist monasteries were thronged with refugees who had assisted in the government of the Sung [Song] empire but would not serve the new alien masters, though at the risk of their lives. The poet Chiang Chieh [Jiang Jie] was one of these. The last character of the Chinese text, "Ming" for "daybreak", was the name adopted by the Chinese restoration in the 14th century.'

Air for the Lute: LPTF, p. 34-35. This version made for 'Two ancient Chinese airs for the lute' with music by Laurence Picken. The following note appears in LPTF: 'The second verse is more literally: "Dreams follow your gold saddle, there is a little sweetness my heart does not put into words: my lute understands the language (for that)." Chinese can express such an idea in far fewer words and syllables than English.'

Snow and Plum: A78, p. 24. R84, p. 186. An earlier version runs as follows:

When plum to snow at spring
  won't yield to favour,
The poet shelves his brush
  or wastes his paper:

For whiteness plum gives snow
  a lead of 'thirty';
For fragrance snow to plum
  must cede the 'tourney';

But as plum without snow
  lacks all its wonder
And snow without a verse
  shows man as vulgar,

At sunset I made this
  (much snow had tumbled)
So with its plum the spring
  might 'make a hundred'!

Farewell to the God of Plagues: LPTF, p. 97. The blood-sucking parasite was the water-borne parasitic disease schistosomiasis (or Bilharzia). Mao celebrates its eradication from a region of the Yangtse valley.

Over Fells So High: Previously unpublished.